Verses Regarding True Nature

and

One Hundred Two Haiku

Bart Marshall

REALFACE PRESS

Published by Realface Press
info@realface.com

ISBN: 978-0-9862035-1-0

Also published by Realface Press:

Christ Sutras: *The Complete Sayings of Jesus from All Sources Arranged into Sermons*, by Bart Marshall

Bhagavad Gita: *The Definitive Translation,* translated by Bart Marshall

The Perennial Way, *Extended Edition,* translated by Bart Marshall

The Triune Self: *Confessions of a Ruthless Seer,* by Mike Snider

Think and Grow Rich, by Napoleon Hill, 80th Anniversary Edition, edited by Bart Marshall

Letters of Transmission: *The Enlightenment Method of Zen Master Alfred Pulyan,* edited by Bart Marshall

After the Absolute, by David Gold with Bart Marshall

Conquest of Illusion, by J.J. van der Leeuw, 90th Anniversary Edition, edited by Bart Marshall

Magic, White and Black, by Franz Hartmann, M.D., edited by Bart Marshall

The Torah: *The Five Books of Moses, King James Readers' Version,* by Bart Marshall

Pearl of the Orient, a screenplay by Bart Marshall

Contents

Verses Regarding True Nature　　　1

One Hundred Two Haiku　　　35

Verses Regarding
True Nature

One

Life goes nowhere and leaves no trace.
It does not begin.
It does not end.
All arises new in the Moment.

Forms and sensations arise in the Moment.
Hopes and plans arise in the Moment.
Memories and artifacts arise in the Moment.

All there is, could be, or could have been
arises in the Moment.
There is only the Moment.

Sit quietly and stop talking to yourself.

Two

The realm of heaven and earth
is created by Awareness.
Universe unfolds in the direction of looking.

Thought creates objects of thought.
Desire creates objects of desire.
Mind creates objects of mind.

Telescopes create galaxies.
Microscopes create atoms.
Travel creates distant lands.

All arise in Awareness.

Awareness is the Source.
Awareness is the Realm.
Awareness is the Witness.

The multitudes appear to be aware,
but then, so do actors on a screen.
What can be said for sure?
Awareness is always and only Here.

Nothing exists without You.
Admit what you see!

Three

When the body dies,
the world dies with it.
Awareness remains ever-present.

The world arises new in the Moment, as always.
Nothing is disturbed.

Four

6

Stories begin and end.

Cling to your story
and you go down with the ship.

Take one step back
and the story cannot touch you.
You are done with beginnings and endings.

Though the ship goes down,
there is no one aboard.

Five

In the Moment, can there be duration?
In the Moment, is movement possible?

The Moment is still, eternal.
Time and motion cause no ripple.
It encompasses the far reaches
and holds them close.
It is the sole realm of Awareness.

There is no escaping it.

Six

The Moment is singular, indivisible, complete.

Images swirl, but the Moment is unmoved.
Time passes, but the Moment goes nowhere.
Forms arise and vanish,
but the Moment is unchanged.

The Moment is eternally still,
yet it cannot be held.
It is all there is or will be.

It does not lead to other moments.

Seven

Absolute, Tao, God, One...
The Source of All has many names.
Names are meaningless.
It is the realm of no-name.

Here, Universe emanates...
Here, Awareness alone exists...
Here, Everything and No-thing are the same...

Here.

Eight

The sage is not different from other men.

Cold wind feels cold.
Things fall apart.
Life grants him no special mercies.

This is fine with him.

Nine

Looking out, Universe is displayed.
What creates Universe?
Looking.

Looking in, Source is perceived.
What creates Source?
Looking creates Source creates Looking.

Ten

12

To know God is impossible.
Nothing stands apart to behold It.
Can you step outside Totality
and take its measure?

To be God is easy.

Stop ignoring the obvious.
Stop pretending to be something else.

Eleven

The sage does not seek students.
Neither does he avoid them.
One who seeks students
needs something from them.
One who avoids them ignores their need.

When students appear,
the sage is happy to teach.
When students are absent,
the sage is happy to be.
The sage is available but not insistent.
He serves but does not strive.

If the student does not seek the teacher,
he must think he already knows.
One who thinks he already knows
is a hopeless case.

Twelve

There is no reason to be busy.
The sage needs little.

Those who want much work hard.
Nothing is ever enough.
Though achievement and wealth
may fill their lives,
their minds are never at rest.

The sage goes about doing nothing.
His glance creates the world.
What more is there to do?

Thirteen

15

The world of appearance is substantial.
Senses tell you it's real.
It is easy to be fooled.

The world of appearance is seductive.
Desire pulls you deep.
It is easy to get lost.

The world of appearance is prison.
Its offerings are shackles.
Freedom seems impossible.

Look close…
It is woven of emptiness!

Fourteen

The Absolute does not punish ignorance
or reward enlightenment.
Ignorance is its own punishment.
Enlightenment leaves no one to reward.

The ignorant grab all they can
and are never satisfied.
They hold tight to their lives,
and cannot rest for fear of dying.

The sage sees nothing worth grabbing.
Life is nothing special.
Death takes nothing from him.

Fifteen

What is the path to the Absolute?
To a wave, which way is the ocean?

In stillness the wave subsides.
What more can be said?

Mind makes waves, as is its nature.
When mind stops, questions end.
There is no need for answers.

The wise student avoids thinking.
He retreats to the close realm
and waits in silence.

Sixteen

To seek knowledge is the nature of the mind.
This is the cause of ignorance.
Without the idea of knowledge,
where is ignorance?

In the world of appearances,
knowledge is useful.
It is useful to know how to cook and knot rope.
Ignorance of practical matters
is overcome by practice.

In the realm of the Absolute,
knowledge is unknown.
Nothing to know, no one to know it.
Ignorance of the Absolute
is overcome by surrender.

Seventeen

There is a saying: "Out of sight, out of mind."
This is common experience.

"Out of mind, out of existence" is also true,
but few understand this.

The sage is like an infant.
He sees the world as Himself
and does not deny it.

Eighteen

In the world of appearances,
the ten thousand things arise and vanish.
Death is the price of birth.

The sage is not immune.
He finds himself in the world
and does not mind.

Joy and contentment fill his days.
Beauty and perfection unfold with every step.
His life is one of great good fortune.

In the end, it will not be missed.

Nineteen

This name that claims you, to what does it refer?
Thoughts, sensations, reflections in mirrors...
Nothing much to stand on.

Without thoughts, what are you?
Without senses, what are you?
With no reflection cast, what are you?

Stop seeking to glorify your name.
Stop seeking to be seen as worthy.
Stop seeking to be known as a knower.

The things you know are not worth knowing.
Worms will eat the thing that knows them.

Twenty

22

The multitudes fear death
and try not to think about it.
When it approaches, panic ensues.

The sage sees death as the companion of life.
He holds it in high regard,
and treats it like a childhood friend.

Death inhabits his thoughts.
Death informs his actions.
Death walks at his side.

When deciding what's worth doing,
he asks the advice of death.

Twenty One

The sage moves in and out of life.

Assuming name and story,
he rides the wind of loss and gain,
blame and praise,
contentment and discontent.

Name and story released, he rests in stillness.

The multitudes know only name and story.
They are at the mercy of the wind,
and know nothing of stillness.

The one with a name is an imposter.
The One with no name is Here.

Twenty Two

There is a saying:
"No matter how far you've gone
in the wrong direction, turn back."
The sage does not teach this.

In a realm of no dimension,
can there be a wrong direction?
In a realm of no dimension,
is movement possible?

There is nowhere you came from,
nowhere you can go.
You are where you are,
no matter how much you travel.

Don't waste time repenting.
Make no effort to be worthy.
Give no thought to absolution.

Drop everything and make good your escape.

Twenty Three

Shadows merge, colors fade.
Darkness has its day but will not last.
Nor will the absence of darkness that follows.

Listen, without straining to hear.
Look, without asking to see.
Seek, without hoping to find.
Illusion can't hold up to scrutiny.

To scrutinize, let go.
Let go of everything.

Twenty Four

26

When the body dies, where is the world?
When you awaken, where is the dream?

Without ears, what is there to hear?
Without eyes, what is there to see?

Look deep.
Listen close.
Without You there is no Creation.

Examine the Moment—there is no time.
Examine the Moment—there is no breath.

Twenty Five

Without leaves and eaves, what sound is wind?

Stillness holds the possibility of movement.
No-thing holds the seed of heaven and earth.

Void becomes Source.
Source becomes Awareness.
Awareness becomes the ten thousand things.
All happens Now, for the first time, forever.

How is this possible?
It's not.
And yet—here it is!

But why care how Universe emanates?
This knowledge is not good for anything.
The sage abides in unknowing
and is unconcerned.

Twenty Six

The world of appearances
is complex, bewildering.
It defies explanation.
Theories and myths are offered,
but there is no agreement.

The multitudes are not bothered by this.
They choose something to believe
and talk endlessly as if they know.

The Source of appearances
is simple, self-evident.
Explanation is not needed or possible.
Though obvious, it is eternal mystery.

The sage is struck dumb by this.
Unknowing is all that he claims.
He is reluctant to break silence.

Belief and ignorance go hand in hand.
The more you think you know,
the farther you are from Truth.

Twenty Seven

The formula for enlightenment is simple.

Inquire within.
Pray for Truth.
Wait in silence.

Inquiry, prayer, no-thought.

Practice with unbending intent
and indifference to outcome.
Heaven will roll at your feet.

Don't say you haven't been told.

Twenty Eight

What do you know for sure?

If one is honest, only this: "Awareness is."
Maybe not even that.

The world within Awareness is elusive.
Some say it's real and vast.
Some say it's a dream in a moment.

The witness of Awareness is in doubt.
Some say it's a person who lives.
Some say it's the deathless One.

The source of Awareness is a mystery.
Some say it arises at birth.
Some say no one's been born.

Nothing is as it seems.
That much is certain.

Twenty Nine

Why is there something rather than nothing?
Awareness.

Presence, Light, Aliveness, God…
It has many names.
Timeless, ever-new —
it can be called Eternal Life.
There is no reason or explanation.
It just is.

It is not ancient—it arises only Now.
It is not distant—it is nearer
than you are to yourself.

It is the substance of Void
and Everything is made of it.

Thirty

The sage knows nothing, yet is always certain.

Certain of what?
The sage does not know.

Unknowable mystery infuses his being,
but nothing is in doubt.

He is free of knowing, therefore he is certain.

Thirty One

The world of appearances is ruthless.

The more you pursue it,
the more enticements it offers.
The more you renounce it,
the more insistent it becomes.

Indifference is the only refuge.

Thirty Two

34

A fearful man is defeated by fear.
A courageous man acts in spite of it.
Without fear, courage cannot arise.
What use is courage to the fearless?

The cause of fear is the unknown.
Unknown outcomes, unknown realms...
Death is the great unknown.
The Truth is also unknown, therefore it is feared.

To seek Truth in earnest takes courage.
The way will pass through death.
The one who seeks it will not survive.
On this, the great masters are unanimous.

One Hundred Two
Haiku

Motionless heron
in still morning shallows.
Death comes with no warning.

Startled awake, utterly still.
I am the trees,
roiling without wind.

Baiting the hook I draw
my own blood.
I catch a fish and let him go.

4

The dream of my self,
no longer believed,
continues unattended.

5

The locust tree that breaks my ax
is where the eagle
lights at sunset.

6

Hidden cove, old trees.
A rotted pier, a sunken boat.
Brown hawks circle.

7

Slack tide at noon.
No wind, clear water.
It is my own self holding still.

8

Always running to
or running from,
arriving is not possible.

9

Dark endless ocean,
swallowing God.
My boat is small and built by hand.

Tire swing, still, on the
grandfather tree. My dead
child's dog startles my hand.

Being dead, I am
as I've been since birth.
Life is not possible here.

Solitude and silence
call me like a mother.
Where is my answer?

When not sitting quietly
doing nothing,
I hurry to return.

13

In silence, my own voice
begs me to listen.
Where is it calling from?

14

Not knowing who I am,
I live life as if.
Death is not fooled by this.

15

41

Straining to hear emptiness,
I am impatient
with interruptions.

Snow trees, morning stove.
Deep in old firewood
burrowed insects burn awake.

Something inside strains
to speak and be heard.
What is it I have to say?

19

The pen, the hand, exist
within me. The thoughts,
the words, come of their own.

20

Against all odds,
it seems, I am.
No reason for it, yet here it is.

21

Quietly being with
nothing to do.
What could be better than this?

43

22

The silent witness,
not doing, not caring,
is whom the world obeys.

23

That face looking out
of the mirror I hold—
who does he think he is?

24

Fresh sheets,
the sound of spring rain.
For a moment I forget I'm dying.

Advance into fear.
Fight for surrender.
Defeat is your victory.

25

Always, the relentless insistence
of the Obvious
to be known.

26

Sudden calm.
There is no reason to believe
I will live out the day.

27

45

Every moment the world
is created from scratch.
This is not a metaphor.

There was never a time
before this.
I never have lived except… Now!

Experiences are so brief.
Does it really matter
what they hold?

Abandon all words.
Without words, what would
there be to misunderstand?

A book falls from the
shelf and opens. It does not
say I am chosen.

No memories or time,
I hurtle through place
on the stillpoint of Now.

34

The wonder is I am at all.
How can I complain
about details?

35

Good man, bad man—
does it matter? I hope not.
I am the worst man I know.

36

I cross with care
the ice-fringed stream.
Falling is unwise so far from home.

37

After a hard-fought defeat,
an all-day rain.
Forgiveness brings the light.

38

Old dying friend,
arms thin as fingers,
asks how my children are doing.

39

Hidden gestures of
secret kindness
dissolve worlds and create anew

49

40

Forgive your enemy,
but do not let on.
Victory will court you.

41

Just now, alone,
cloistered by rain,
on a porch overlooking water…

42

Old cove of childhood, here again.
At the moment of looking,
fish jump.

43

To fight or to bow
is seldom clear. I ask,
"Which will strengthen my heart?"

44

Swirling trees with no wind.
Agreement
after long misunderstanding.

45

A good man deflects credit,
shoulders blame.
Why do so few embrace this?

51

The thrill of existence
is unknown
to the Creator of all things.

Dark morning house,
quiet open windows.
Coffee, and the scent of Truth.

Pancakes and eggs
in an all-night diner.
The waitress touches my hand.

49

How strange he is,
this one who thinks he's me.
Where does he go when I sleep?

50

When it is time to
write and no poetry comes,
you must change your life.

51

Spring days in January.
Daffodils and spirits
are fooled to life.

53

In stillness, songs
of the ten-thousand things
sung by a lone mockingbird.

Night wind at the window,
an old lover's voice.
I make my confession.

Cold sun, thin winter sky.
Shards of razor-edged light
assemble the world.

Night winter rain,
my daughter hours late.
The sudden phone stops my heart.

56

Long black night of unstoppable
thought. Sleep never comes.
Dawn greys the sky.

57

Bare woods, sharp shadows.
The lines of the world
intermingle as branches.

58

Thinking and doing,
I live out my scarce days.
Ceasing, I erase death.

59

Churning out dreams,
unearthing desires,
the flywheel holds momentum.

60

At dawn I rise to the day.
Night comes, it seems,
but a few thoughts later.

I am, therefore thought happens.
From Nothing, a thought,
therefore I am.

For a moment of glory,
years of work.
Better to glory in work.

Fearful and worried, I am old.
Lost in laughter,
I am yet unborn.

Distilled thought, frozen glimpse,
plain statement of truth—
Haiku are not hidden.

Good friends no longer young.
How grateful we've become
for the privilege.

When I die
the world dies with me.
In consciousness alone it exists.

67

Unending fear, lust,
toil and devouring.
Hell is not elsewhere.

68

After death we are remembered,
vaguely,
by others who soon perish.

69

Thinking of battle conjures fear.
When fighting the battle,
there is neither fear nor thinking.

The aching beauty
of this poignant world
is felt only by contrast.

Life dissipates
and is forgotten.
How can it be of consequence?

True gratitude of heart
does not bargain,
or ask for further mercies.

The dam has burst.
I no longer look outside myself
for anything.

The world is not viewed
through the one with eyes.
To see clearly, what a thing!

Knowledge breeds with
knowledge and multiplies.
Truth awaits your emptiness.

Sitting quietly, doing nothing.
Thoughts come or don't come
as they please.

Without technique, only sit.
Meditation
teaches meditation.

Choose carefully your words.
Even great poems and sutras
pollute silence.

Masters say, "Look within."
But where is within
when there is no without?

It is not two,
the stark Absolute,
the softness of oblivion.

As everything I am and know
perishes,
who is the witness?

82

Religions feed ignorance
in God's name.
The Truth is best sought elsewhere.

83

Dark morning window,
lighted room. Looking out
I see only within.

84

Sudden emptiness of mind.
He has vanished,
the one who is not God.

Simplify desires.
Fulfillment comes from
recognizing you are full.

The pain I endure,
and enjoy,
is all in service of vanity.

Warm winter wind, so unexpected.
I forget my complaints,
and breathe.

Child of my child,
so perfect and true, what brings
you to these arms and heart?

Do without expecting.
Receive without claiming.
Everything comes.

Empty mind,
gazing between, not at,
sees Nothing with great clarity.

Advancing age means little.
I am growing old,
but becoming young.

To stop completely
and only be
flings wide the doors of perception.

The one who stands behind
and merely watches
has taken center stage.

Father, forgive me.
I am but a sick and whining child
in your house.

Quiet days are best.
There is a tyranny to
special occasions.

Too busy for haiku,
I write one anyway.
It looks much like this.

No history or future.
All there ever was or will be
is Here.

Open window,
trees faint-tipped red.
Just this, and winter is forgotten.

So many lists
of things to fix and do,
so few moments of clear life.

If the world is not real,
which it is not,
why bother to improve it?

Once awake,
does it really matter whether
the dream was good or bad?

Grey morning, wet spring trees.
The seeking of Truth
is what keeps it hidden.

About the Author

The author lives in hiding
and continues to claim
his innocence.